THE
POCKET

LOUIS
VUITTON

Published in 2025
by Gemini Books
Part of Gemini Books Group

Based in Woodbridge and London

Marine House, Tide Mill Way,
Woodbridge, Suffolk IP12 1AP
United Kingdom

www.geminibooks.com

Text and Design © 2025 Gemini Adult Books Ltd
Part of the Gemini Pockets series

Text by Laia Farran Graves
Cover illustration by Caroline Andrieu

ISBN 978-1-80247-289-9

A CIP catalogue record for this book is available from the British Library.

Disclaimer: This book is solely intended for general informational and
entertainment purposes only. Any trademarks, copyright, gameshows,
company names, registered names, products, individuals, logos
and catchphrases used or cited in this book are the property of their
respective owners and for identity, review and guidance purpose only.
This book is a publication of the Pocket Gemini series of books by
Gemini Adult Books Ltd, part of Gemini Books Group and has not been
licensed, approved, associated with, sponsored or endorsed by Louis
Vuitton, any person or entity.

Printed in China

10 9 8 7 6 5 4 3 2 1

FSC
MIX
Paper | Supporting
responsible forestry
FSC® C020056
www.fsc.org

Picture Credits: Alamy Stock Photo: Grzegorz Czapski 4, 8, 38, 46; Peter
Horree 33. Getty Images: Geoffroy Van Der Hasselt 58; Julien De Rosa 90;
Pascal Le Segretain 77; Penske Media 70; Victor Chavez 95.

THE POCKET

LOUIS VUITTON

G:

LOUIS VUITTON

CONTENTS

INTRODUCTION

Founded in Paris in 1854, Louis Vuitton started as a family business specializing in luggage. The first to create trunks with a flat lid, rather than rounded, to enable stacking, Vuitton also developed new, waterproof fabrics with which to line them, in place of animal skins.

In 1896, Georges Vuitton, Louis Vuitton's son, designed one of the most iconic prints to date: the Monogram. In 1901, the Maison launched its first handbag and more styles followed – the Sac Marin (1927), the Speedy and the Keepall (1930) and the Noé (1932). By now, stores had had opened around the world.

In 1997, Marc Jacobs was appointed to design the first ready-to-wear clothing for women. He was superseded by Nicolas Ghesquière in 2013. A decade later, Pharrell Williams became Creative Director for menswear, following the death of Virgil Abloh in 2021. Today, Louis Vuitton remains one of the most renowned and luxurious brands in the world.

"What I have in mind are things that are deluxe but that you can also throw into a bag and escape town with, because Louis Vuitton has a heritage in travel."

MARC JACOBS,
VOGUE, JUNE 2012

CHAPTER ONE

EARLY YEARS

LUXURY AT ITS FINEST

This luxurious and internationally acclaimed French Maison was founded by Monsieur Louis Vuitton in 1854. It was first known as Louis Vuitton Malletier (*malletier* is French for "trunk-maker"), as it specialized in luggage. The global brand, which currently has more than 460 stores over 50 different countries, is now part of Moët Hennessy Louis Vuitton (LVMH), the world's largest luxury goods empire.

A RANGE OF PRODUCTS

In addition to its original offering, Louis Vuitton now provides a range of products, including prêt-à-porter collections, leather goods and accessories (shoes, perfume, watches and jewellery and an exquisite collection of hard-cover books).

HUMBLE BEGINNINGS

Louis Vuitton was born on 4 August 1821 in the village of Anchay, located in the Jura region of eastern France. His mother died when he was only ten years old, and although his father remarried, he too died soon afterwards. When Louis was 13, he left home with the objective of reaching Paris, and walked across France taking occasional jobs until he reached the capital in 1837.

TRADING PLACES

Once in Paris, the young Louis became an apprentice at a box-making and packing workshop – a very sought-after profession at the time, as horse-drawn carriages were very popular among affluent members of society. *Layetiers, emballeurs* and *malletiers* (box-makers, packers and luggage-makers) were very much in demand to help the wealthy transport their belongings on their various journeys.

Louis Vuitton's mentor was Monsieur Romain Maréchal, a recognized tradesman whose workshop was located on the prestigious Rue Saint-Honoré. As was customary at the time, Vuitton worked there for several years until he branched out on his own.

HIGH SOCIETY

Many of Vuitton's clients at M. Maréchal's studio were members of the French aristocracy who loved to travel between their many residences, and in 1853 Louis Vuitton was appointed the position of personal packer to the Empress of the French, Eugénie de Montijo. She was married to Emperor Napoleon III (nephew of Napoleon I) and was a very influential figure and trendsetter in the world of fashion.

SETTING UP SHOP

Louis Vuitton married Clemence-Emilie Parriaux – who was 17 at the time – on 22 April 1854. That same year the couple opened their first Parisian store and workshop, located at 4 Rue Neuve-des-Capucines, near the Place Vendôme. They placed a sign outside that read: "Securely packs the most fragile objects. Specializing in packing fashions."

THE FIRST INNOVATIONS

Trunks in this era were usually made from animal skin (pig's skin and other leathers) and were not waterproof. They were also made with rounded tops to allow water to run down in the event of a downpour. Louis Vuitton recognized the restrictions these options offered and, ever the problem-solver, in 1865 he designed a water-resistant version in a lightweight canvas that was treated with glue. This trunk had been commissioned by Empress Eugénie, who chose to have it made to match her salons in a light shade of grey, a colour that soon became known as Trianon grey. This was seen as very innovative, at a time when most trunks were either black or brown.

Louis Vuitton also recognized that the weight of the trunks would sometimes pose a problem. In his quest to reduce it, he used treated canvas instead of the heavier leathers, and a lightweight poplar wood to make the frames, which he then reinforced with attractive beechwood.

STACKING UP!

In 1858, Vuitton designed his first Steamer Trunk, which had a flat lid for easy stacking. Coinciding with the dawn of passenger transatlantic crossings, they soon became very popular, and as his business grew he expanded into a new workshop near Paris at 18 Rue de Congrès, Asnières, where he employed 20 people. He lived there with his family, in a flat above the studio, until he built his large new home in the grounds.

EARLY FAME

In 1867, Louis Vuitton was awarded a bronze medal for his designs at the acclaimed Exposition Universelle, Paris. He was highly innovative in his ideas, but was also true to his heritage and precise execution, using traditional methods of craftsmanship. This brought him great recognition, and such was his fame at this point in the story of the Maison, that he was creating luggage for exclusive customers – including heads of state such as Isma'il Pasha, the Khedive of Egypt.

LOUIS VUITTON IN ASNIÈRES

The historic family home of Vuitton is an impressive Art Nouveau building. Today the premises include a working atelier, where 170 employees still produce custom-made special orders and trunks for select clients, and a gallery space that hosts the Maison's shows and events.

ARRIVAL IN PARIS

During the Franco-Prussian War (1870–71), Louis Vuitton's workshop was looted and destroyed, but he was able to rebuild it in peacetime. In 1871, he opened a new shop in Paris at 1 Rue Scribe, Opéra, which operated as the Louis flagship store until 1914.

A FAMILY AFFAIR

Louis and Clemence-Emilie Vuitton had a son together called Georges (1857–1936). When he was 16 he became an apprentice at the Asnières workshop, and later managed the Maison's flagship store, freeing his father up to work on new, exciting designs. Louis Vuitton died on 27 February 1892, and Georges inherited his father's business.

GLOBAL BEGINNINGS

Like his father, George Vuitton had a good business sense, but he also had a global vision for the brand. He opened a store in London's Oxford Street as early as 1885, and in 1893 decided to exhibit at the Chicago World's Fair in the United States. He was the only French luggage vendor to attend and completely sold out of stock.

While at the fair, he was introduced to the American businessman John Wanamaker who later sold Louis Vuitton luggage items in his department store, introducing the brand to the US market.

SPREADING THE WORD

In 1914, Georges launched the new flagship store on the Champs-Élysées. It would become the largest luggage store in the world and the Parisian elite, including Coco Chanel, became regular customers. The brand continued to expand, and more shops opened in cities across the world, including New York, Washington D.C., Bombay and Buenos Aires.

CLASSIC COLLECTIBLES

Georges Vuitton was known for his love of cars, which led him to create a collection of trunks designed for automobiles. First shown at trade shows in 1897, the trunks were made out of a canvas lining that he called Vuittonite, and designed to match the car in which they would travel. As a novelty, these trunks ranged from lunch and tea cases, to toiletry bags, pharmacy trunks and tool boxes, and could be placed in different sections of the vehicle, including the overhead rack.

AERO TRAVEL

Inspired by the new forms of travel, Georges Vuitton also designed the Aero Trunk in 1906. This piece of luggage was made to go in the gondola of a hot-air balloon and in a helicopter prototype, which had been designed by his ingenious twin sons, Jean and Pierre. The Aero was developed further, and by 1927 it became the Maison's most popular trunk.

THE NEXT GENERATIONS

Georges Vuitton died on 26 October 1936, aged 79, leaving his eldest son Gaston-Louis Vuitton in charge of the company. Both twin sons had sadly died (in 1910 and 1917) and the family business was now in the hands of the only heir.

Gaston-Louis (1883–1970), who was known as "the collector of objects", took the Maison into new, uncharted territory by expanding its offerings; and in 1914, he rebranded Louis Vuitton with the strapline, "Manufacturer of trunks, leather goods, goldsmith products and travel items".

LVMH

Gaston-Louis Vuitton died in 1970, and in 1977, Odile Vuitton (the great-granddaughter of Louis Vuitton) inherited the business. Her husband, the businessman Henri Racamier, took charge of the brand with a focus on its global expansion, resulting in the opening of 100 stores worldwide over the next ten years.

Then, in 1984, as recommended by
Racamier's financial director Joseph Lafont,
the once family-owned company went public.
Louis Vuitton merged with luxury champagne
brand Moët et Chandon, and with spirits
company Hennessy three years later, in
1987, becoming the hugely successful luxury
conglomerate that is LVMH. The company
currently owns over 75 prestigious, luxury
brands across six major market sectors.

LOUIS VUITTON CANVAS

After the introduction of the Trianon grey canvas in 1865, Louis Vuitton worked on several other patterns, including a striped one called Rayée. It was designed in 1872 in red and beige, and a tan and beige version followed in 1876.

A trademarked, check print called Damier was also available from 1888, when it was designed by both Louis and his son Georges. The check included the words "Marque L. Vuitton Déposée" ("L. Vuitton Registered Trademark") as a response to the large number of Louis Vuitton copies that were being made even then.

In 1896, Georges Vuitton designed the legendary Louis Vuitton Monogram print in memory of his late father. It too was designed in an attempt to deter copycats.

THE MONOGRAM

The Monogram has become so recognizable internationally that it is now synonymous with the Maison, and is an integral part of its design code. The distinct pattern has rows of quatrefoil flowers in three different versions and in two shades of brown, and Louis Vuitton's initials, "LV". Some say that Georges Vuitton's inspiration for the print comes from the tiles in the kitchen of his family's house at Asnières, others claim it reflected the trend in Asian art at the time.

IN DEMAND

Many bags were designed under Georges Vuitton's watch, including the Squire – later renamed the Alma – a domed bag requested by Coco Chanel in 1925. Due to its success, more followed, including the Keepall and the Speedy (AKA the Express), in 1930. These could be folded when travelling, making them both practical and versatile. In 1932 came the Noé (designed by Gaston-Louis Vuitton to carry five champagne bottles) and in 1966 the cylindrical Papillon was launched.

AN UNPICKABLE LOCK

Apart from being a skilled trunk-maker and a visionary designer, Louis Vuitton was very good at making locks. In 1886, he designed a mechanism that became known as the unpickable lock (and is still in use today), to protect the contents of his customers' luggage. The new device was patented, and had two spring buckles and a registered single key that was numbered, and would be assigned to each client regardless of the amount of suitcases or trunks that she or he owned.

Louis and his son felt so strongly about the efficacy of this mechanism that they publicly challenged Harry Houdini (the famed American escape artist), to free himself from a locked Louis Vuitton trunk. It is said that he declined this offer.

HALLMARKS OF AUTHENTICITY

Louis Vuitton's exceptionally crafted items have been the source of counterfeits since the 1800s, when they were first created. Concerned by this, Louis and Georges first responded by trademarking their unique canvas designs. In today's market, with the rise of super-fakes, it is advised that you purchase your Louis Vuitton goods from reputable stores, or auction houses if you are opting for second-hand goods. It is also recommended you seek advice from an authenticating expert if purchasing items on the preloved market.

VINTAGE VUITTON

Genuine Louis Vuitton's products are never sold at discounted prices in-store. If you are seeking a second-hand item that is still in production, it is a good idea to check the design on their website, as the positioning of the pattern is very precise (for example, on a Neverfull Damier canvas Grande Modèle bag, the logo sits on the sixth square from the top). When inspecting a piece, bear in mind that Louis Vuitton is a luxury brand and it should feel as such when you hold it, zip it up or simply touch it.

CHAPTER TWO

KEY PIECES

THE STEAMER TRUNK

Many trunk styles were developed by the Maison over the years, adapting to the changing needs of passengers. The Louis Vuitton Steamer, first introduced in 1858, is considered by many to be the most iconic trunk of all times. It is often seen used as an elegant coffee table (by adding a thick sheet of glass on the top) or as a chic storage unit.

In French these trunks were called Malles Courrier (Mail Trunks). The name derives from the fact that they would leave at the same time as the mail, whether on a steam train or an ocean liner.

THE WARDROBE TRUNK

This piece was introduced in 1875, and soon became a must-have among travellers. The Malle Armoire opened into two halves, usually with a rail and hangers on one side (the hangers were called "princess" hangers), and drawers on the other. These could be, of course, customized to specific requirements and to accommodate different wardrobes. A version for gentlemen, known as the Ideal Trunk, or Malle Idéale, became very popular when it was first introduced in 1905.

Other trunk variations to store clothes included the Malle Chemise, or Shirt Trunk, and the Commode, or Trouser Trunk, which as the titles suggest, were designed to accommodate a single type of garment.

THE BED TRUNK

Another functional trunk, the Bed Trunk, was designed in the 1860s with explorers in mind. Ingeniously, it opened to reveal a foldable bed with a lined mattress, adjustable legs and two headboards – one at the top and one at the base. The explorer Pierre Savorgnan de Brazza commissioned several Bed Trunks, the first of which was designed in 1875, as well as some zinc and copper trunks (made of metal to protect the trunk's contents from possible severe weather conditions and from insects) for his lengthy three-year expedition to Africa.

THE FLOWER TRUNK

During the great flood of Paris in 1910, the water level of the river Seine rose 26 feet (8 metres), causing a great deal of damage and disruption. Due to this emergency, Louis Vuitton and his son Gaston were unable to deliver all the orders that had been placed by customers, and as a gesture of goodwill, and to thank them for their patience (and as a clever marketing ploy), they sent them each a zinc-lined trunk with flowers inside.

This trunk, the Malle Fleurs, was later gifted by the Maison to pregnant customers, and is available today to purchase from the Louis Vuitton website.

LIBRARY & DESK TRUNKS

Library Trunks became very popular for customers setting off on long journeys, and allowed them to take entire book collections with them to pass the time. These trunks, when opened, comprised shelves or drawers for the books, and sometimes even included a foldable desk (as in the case of the Malle Bureau or Desk Trunk).

The best known trunk in this category is probably the Stokowski Trunk, designed in the 1930s for the renowned conductor. It became his travel companion when on tour, and included a desk, drawers and shelves to hold his music scores and other paperwork.

Another outstanding Desk Trunk was designed in 1927 by Gaston-Louis Vuitton for the American novelist Ernest Hemingway. It included seven drawers to accommodate books and documents, as well as shelves, secret drawers and a main drawer to hold a typewriter. The trunk went missing at one stage, and was eventually found in 1944 in the basement of The Ritz hotel in Paris. Inside was the long-lost manuscript of his novel, *A Moveable Feast* (1964). This legendary piece is now known as the Hemingway Library Trunk.

THE ALZER SUITCASE

Around 1875, the Maison – in keeping with the latest travel innovations – began designing garment bags and suitcases. Their first design was the Porte-habits Rigide and later, in 1892, the Porte-habits á Soufflet, a softer version.

During the 1950s, as flying became a more accessible form of travel, the Alzer suitcase, still in production today, was launched and became a must-have among frequent air travellers. It was available in several sizes and finishes, some of which have since been discontinued. Many were also customized – and all are very sought-after at auction or in the vintage market.

TRAVEL BAGS & HANDBAGS

The first hand-luggage to be introduced by Louis Vuitton was the Steamer Bag, designed in 1901. It was often used as a laundry bag when on long boat or car journeys. The bag could be folded flat when not in use, making it extremely practical.

"I love working at Louis Vuitton. I love fashion. That's why I do it. No one's forcing me to do this. And nobody forces anyone to buy it. It's a real love affair."

MARC JACOBS, *VOGUE*, DECEMBER 2011

LOUIS VUITTON

THE SPEEDY

The legendary Louis Vuitton Speedy was
designed in 1930. Originally known as the
Express, it was 12 inches (30 cm) in length
and was made in plain leather, with a padlock
attached. A year later it was manufactured
in the classic Monogram canvas pattern and
became very popular.

The Speedy was available in three sizes, and in
1965, at Audrey Hepburn's request, a smaller
version was made: this variant was 10 inches
(25 cm) long and is still available today. It
became an instant classic. Other celebrity
fans of this bag at the time were Jackie
Kennedy, Lauren Bacall, Sophia Loren and
Catherine Deneuve.

The bag's canvas has been redesigned by a number of artists over time, including Stephen Sprouse (in 2001, and in 2009 in a tribute collection designed by Marc Jacobs), by Takashi Murakami (from 2003–15) and Yayoi Kusama (in 2012 and 2023).

THE ALMA

The dome-shaped Alma, with its art deco references and bold silhouette, is another iconic piece in the Louis Vuitton handbag collection. It has a wide, flat, sturdy base, two Toron handles, a leather key tag and a gold padlock and key. It is fitted with a detachable and adjustable strap.

THE NOÉ

The Louis Vuitton bucket bag with the drawstring closure was introduced in 1932, originally created to carry five bottles of champagne. There have been many variations and sizes over the years, but the adjustable straps and roomy size make it a beloved and practical choice.

THE KEEPALL

Launched in the 1930s, the Keepall is a large-capacity, foldable weekend or airline cabin bag. It was designed by Gaston-Louis Vuitton to offer more flexible luggage options and provide an alternative to hard suitcases. Some models have cross-body or shoulder straps, and it is available in canvas, coated canvas and embossed leather, as well as many limited editions.

THE CAPUCINES

Named after the Rue Neuve-des-Capucines in Paris, the site of Louis Vuitton's first shop, this elegant leather bag has a semi-rigid handle and a flap over the top that can be folded to reveal the "LV" initials, or, the monogrammed flower. The Artycapucines collaboration, which began in 2019, was a limited edition range by celebrated artists, such as Liza Lou, Ziping Wang, Tursic & Mille and Ewa Juszkiewicz, who imbued the iconic model with their own visions.

THE NEVERFULL

A practical tote, the Neverfull, was released in 2007, and has become one of the most recognizable items from the Maison, as well as one of their best-selling. This bag can carry up to 200 pounds (91 kg) and, as described on the Louis Vuitton website, it is creative, elegant, practical and iconic – and referred to as the epitome of effortless elegance and versatility.

The Neverfull is available in three different sizes (PM Petit Modèle, MM Moyen Modèle and GM Grande Modèle), making it practical for everyday use. It is usually seen in the classic Monogram or the Damier canvas, but special limited editions are also available. Hilary Duff, Katie Holmes and Diane Kruger are among the many fans of this classic icon.

A DEDICATED CLIENTELE

Louis Vuitton is today an established global luxury business, but its international success is not only due to novel designs, impeccable execution and a deep understanding of its customers, but also to its prowess in branding.

Through the decades the company has excelled in attracting the best clients. In 1928, the Indian Maharajas became important customers, and in 1938 King George VI and his wife Elizabeth commissioned some suitcases for a pair of dolls belonging to the future Queen Elizabeth II and her sister Margaret.

CELEBRITY STATUS

Louis Vuitton's quality and simple designs, as well as its heritage, has appealed to many, and during the 1950s and 1960s a growing number of glamorous celebrities were spotted carrying its luggage, becoming supporters and unofficial ambassadors of the Maison – something Louis Vuitton encouraged.

Famous followers of the Louis Vuitton brand during this period:

- Catherine Deneuve and her then husband David Bailey

- Juliette Greco

- Anna Magnani (famously photographed in Paris in 1960 next to her Louis Vuitton luggage collection)

- Brigitte Bardot

- Audrey Hepburn

- Lauren Bacall (whose Louis Vuitton initialled luggage collection was sold at auction for $37,000 in 2015)

CHAPTER THREE

FASHION
COLLECTIONS

ON THE RUNWAY

Louis Vuitton's fashion collections were introduced in March 1998, with the first prêt-à-porter collection for women under the recently appointed Marc Jacobs.

While staying true to the brand's spirit of travelling and its roots in luggage-making, the fashion collections designed by Marc Jacobs have captivated audiences and shaped the fashion landscape over the decades.

THE DEBUT COLLECTION

Marc Jacobs debuted at Louis Vuitton for Autumn/Winter 1998 with a collection that was timeless and outstanding in equal measure. A simple colour palette of blues, denim, purple, white and black with a feminine silhouette that had a hint of Prada's classic tailoring, delighted the fashion industry and beyond.

His updated version of standard silhouettes of the 1950s set the bar high, consolidating the brand as a firm regular on the Paris Fashion Week schedule. Kate Moss and Naomi Campbell were among the models who walked in his first show.

THE GRAFFITI COLLECTION

This show for Spring/Summer 2001 started with five male models holding a selection of trunks and cases from the Stephen Sprouse Graffiti collection of that year. As they left the runway, the rest of the collection began with a presentation of ladylike, very feminine summery looks, which included white, black, red, green, navy blue and some floral prints.

There were some military influences as well as stripes and sailor hats. Shoes were mostly flat with some high and mid-heels.

"The combination of the staid, old-school Vuitton luggage and the unique energy of Sprouse's most typical, purest work makes both Sprouse and the luggage look somehow fresh."

TAMA JANOWITZ,
VOGUE, 2001

AFTER DARK

The controversial Spring/Summer 2008 show was inspired by Richard Prince's *Nurse* paintings, one of which was the cover of a Sonic Youth album. Twelve models (including Stephanie Seymour, Naomi Campbell, Eva Herzigová and Nadja Auermann) were dressed in looks that hinted at nurse uniforms, with see-through plastic coats and black lace masks, and hats that together spelled LOUIS VUITTON.

The rest of the show was colourful and playful, with contrasting textures in fun, bright colours, such as vibrant purple and orange, yellow and blue. There were also floor-length looks to finish the show in various necklines – off the shoulder, strapless and low-cut, which were accessorized with long gloves and hair pieces.

AND GOD CREATED WOMAN

For Autumn/Winter 2010, Marc Jacobs took inspiration from 1950s and 1960s femininity and the starlet Brigitte Bardot, bringing cinched-in waists and circle skirts to the runway. With a focus on the breasts instead of the legs, there were perky ponytails, block-heeled pumps and a range of Speedy bags with satin, sequins, metallic thread and fur.

FETISH COLLECTION

This provocative collection for Autumn/Winter 2011 was the talk of the town, with Kate Moss closing the show wearing high-waisted, tailored, black hot pants, a sexy ornate jacket and lace-up boots, while smoking a cigarette (on No Smoking Day, no less...).

The atmospheric set was made to look like a hotel, with doormen opening and closing the heavy brass handles on the glass doors of lifts, as the girls (including Amber Valletta and Naomi Campbell) walked out wearing plenty of patent leather, sheer fabrics, skirts with suspenders and Peter Pan collars over cashmere pieces.

LE CARROUSEL

For this mesmerizing Spring/Summer 2012 show, the curtain was raised to reveal an all-white carousel with 48 models sitting on horses. As the fairground attraction started to go round, one by one, the girls slid off their respective horses and walked delicately in their peep-toe shoes – some with metallic detailing – around the catwalk, wearing 1960s-inspired looks in soft pastel colours, the colour of sugared almonds.

Accessorized with transparent bags, they embodied the epitome of Parisian elegance. Music from Heszékeny, Goblin and William Orbit created a truly magical atmosphere.

ALL ABOARD THE LOUIS VUITTON EXPRESS

One of the most spectacular shows Paris has ever seen was Louis Vuitton's Autumn/ Winter 2012 presentation. This stunning show recreated a railway station, with its traditional ironwork and a large clock, over a marquee in a courtyard of the Louvre Museum. The set also featured an impressive steam train, built from scratch for the occasion, that pulled into the "Louis Vuitton station". Once the train had arrived, the models emerged from the carriage and disembarked wearing platform heels and large hats that had been designed by British milliner Stephen Jones, creating imposing silhouettes. Porters, of course, carried the passengers' Louis Vuitton luggage.

Front row guests included Sarah Jessica Parker, Kanye West and Natalia Vodianova.

"[A] turn of the century feel, but with bits of the 1960s and 1970s. It's not about researching a specific period. It's about having romantic notions of an era and making it beautiful. It doesn't matter if the looks in your head never existed before. That's good."

MARC JACOBS,
THE *GUARDIAN*, MARCH 2012

ANIME

Referencing Wong Kar-wai's movie *2046*,
Minecraft and the anime series *Evangelion*,
the Spring/Summer 2016 collection was
created while Nicolas Ghesquière was Creative
Director of womenswear. It featured black
and pink biker jackets, laser-cut vests and
metal embroidery, embodying the virtual
world of gaming.

"I think if you don't put yourself in aesthetic danger every season, you're not playing the game of fashion."

NICOLAS GHESQUIÈRE,
VOGUE'S THE RUN-THROUGH PODCAST

STREET & SPORTS

For Autumn/Winter 2016, the set was an underwater world, a lost Atlantis with 57 columns of shattered mirrors, made in collaboration with the French artist Justin Morin. There were sporty racing stripes, storm flaps, harnesses, bondage trousers and zips mixed with sensual dresses in scarf prints and sequins.

RETRO FUTURISM

With the entrance as the I. M. Pei-designed glass pyramid of the Louvre, and the show staged at the Pavillon de l'Horloge, which is presided over by the Great Sphinx of Tanis, the Spring/Summer 2018 show featured Ghesquière's typical time-travel. There were embellished coats, sequinned dresses and space-age trainers lending a retro-futuristic vibe.

ART WORLD

For Autumn/Winter 2021, Ghesquière drew
on the playful mid-century paintings by Piero
Fornasetti to create an intersection of the
past and present. Ancient Roman, Greek and
Etruscan sculptures in the Louvre's Denon
wing served as a backdrop to Daft Punk's
mega-hit "Around the World". Craftsmanship
and technology, history and hipness were
evident in the cocoon shapes, surface detailing
and jewel colours. Due to the Covid-19
restrictions, this was a digital show, finishing
with the last model looking up at the statue
Winged Victory of Samothrace.

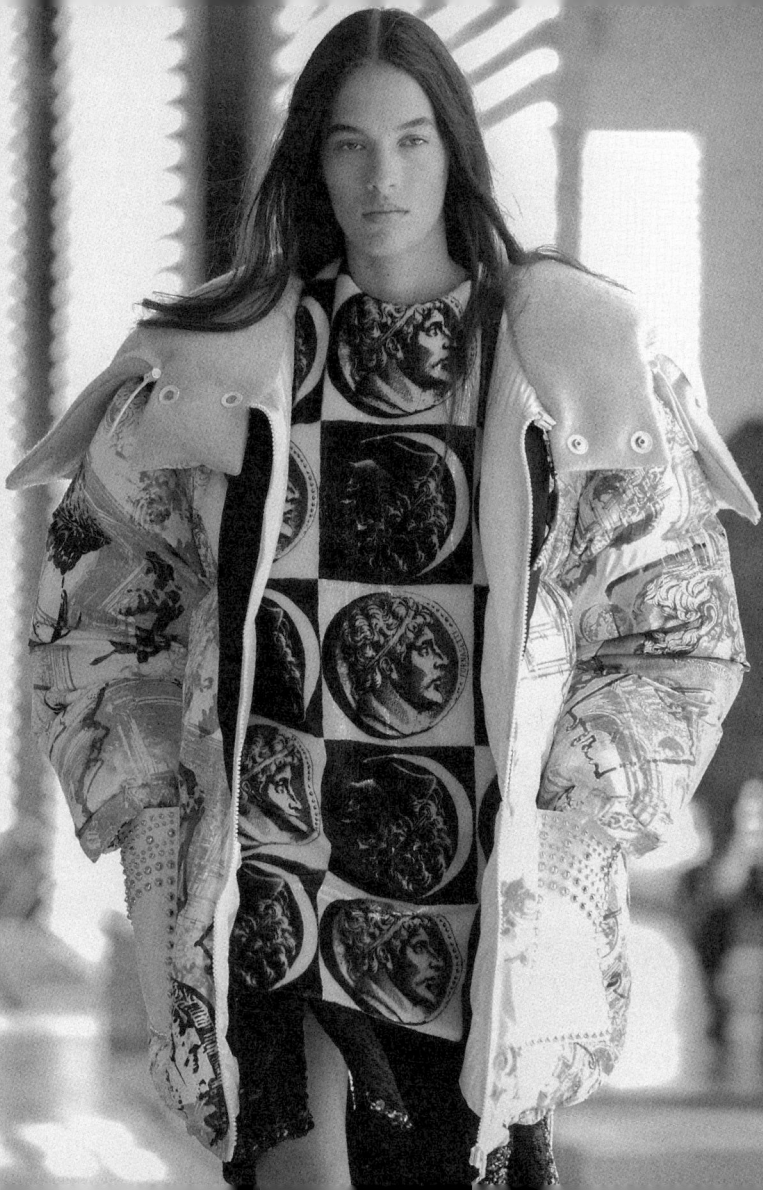

CHANDELIERS & BALLROOMS

Antique chandeliers in the Louvre's Passage Richelieu (according to legend this space was used by Louis Vuitton for his meetings with Empress Eugénie) set an opulent ballroom theme for a magical Spring/Summer 2022 show. Embellished dresses with extreme panniers and layered underskirts referenced 19th-century style, while capes ranged in style from frayed chiffon to polka dots.

"I want to make a proposition that will touch people; not everyone can wear the bags or the shoes or the clothes but they can share the emotion with us."

NICOLAS GHESQUIÈRE,
VOGUE, OCTOBER 2024

THE DAMOFLAGE DEBUT

Pharrell William's first show for Louis Vuitton was his Men's Spring/Summer 2024 collection, featuring the house's Damier check, with a special pixellated version on all manner of clothes, shoes and bags. Models drove golf carts hauling oversized Louis Vuitton trunks.

"... what you get is an amazing team of 55 departments, 2,500 master artisans, resources to do whatever it is that you envisage. You never really hear, 'No.'"

PHARRELL WILLIAMS,
ON WORKING AT LOUIS VUITTON,
GQ, JUNE 2023

LE MONDE EST À VOUS (THE WORLD IS YOUR OYSTER)

By selecting such a symbolic choice of venue – the gardens at the UNESCO building in the French capital – Pharell Williams was all about using the Louis Vuitton platform in the Spring/ Summer 2025 show to promote diversity. A mixed casting "from the Blackest of the Black to the whitest of the white" was also integral to the theme of unity, with clothes varied in tone to match each model's natural skin tone.

The collection was energized and elegant; it featured tailoring and elevated streetwear to a new level. It showcased versatile garments such as wide trousers and leather jackets, but also bags and trunks, reinforcing the travelling element that is at the heart of the Maison.

A SPORTY YEAR

With the Paris Olympics about to start and the Euro 2024 football championships underway, there were – of course – many sports references (shirts branded with a LVFC logo and a football-shaped bag) as well as streetwear with athleisure garments. Williams also successfully reworked the branding that has been such a substantial part of the history of the Maison, not only in the collection, but also in the setting – the grass was cut in checks (like the Damier print) and the print on the bags and many of the garments was updated (featuring new colours and sizes).

"[The show was] about unity and the oneness of what one could look like when you just invite everybody in as a whole."

PHARRELL WILLIAMS,
ON HIS MEN'S SPRING/SUMMER 2025 COLLECTION,
LE MONDE EST Á VOUS, JUNE 2024

VUITTON ON FILM

Any piece by Louis Vuitton is a recognizable status symbol, and as such there have been many key appearances in various films over time. Here are some of the most noteworthy:

FASHION COLLECTIONS

1. The Monogram luggage set in
The Darjeeling Limited (2007)

2. The Keepall in *Death Becomes Her* (1992)

3. The Murakami cherry blossom Pochette
Accessoires in *Mean Girls* (2004)

4. The Motard Firebird from *Sex and the
City* (2008)

5. Louis Vuitton vintage luggage in *Coming
to America* (1988)

6. More Louis Vuitton luggage in the James
Bond movie, *A View to a Kill* (1985)

7. The Monogram Steamer bag in
Charade (1963)

8. Even more Louis Vuitton luggage in
Nine (2009)

9. The Capucines bag in *Cruella* (2021)

THE "LV" RAP

Considering the status of the Louis Vuitton brand, it is no surprise that the Maison should be found in many musical lyrics, and in particular in hip-hop. Here are just a few of the key songs:

1. Sir Mix-a-Lot, 'Swap Meet Louie' (1992)
2. 50 Cent, 'Ghetto Qur'an' (1999)
3. Cam'ron, 'Soap Opera' (2004)
4. Kanye West, 'Last Call' (2004)
5. Kanye West, 'Stronger' (2007)
6. Jay Z, 'Jockin' Jay-Z' (2008)
7. Kanye West, 'I'm The Shit (Remix)' (2009)

8. Big Sean, 'Fat Raps (Remix)' (2010)

9. Wale, 'Lotus Flower Bomb' (2011)

10. 2 Chainz, 'Birthday Song' (2012)

11. A$AP Rocky, 'Pretty Flacko (Remix)' (2012)

12. Skepta, 'That's Not me' (2014)

13. Lil Uzi Vert, 'Seven Million' (2016)

14. Travis Scott, 'High Fashion' (2016)

15. Playboi Carti, 'Run it Up' (2019)

16. Griselda, 'Scotties' (2019)

17. Pop Smoke, 'Christopher Walking' (2020)

18. Lil Durk and Gunna, 'What Happened to Virgil' (2022)

19. Tyler, the Creator and Nigo, 'Come on, Let's Go' (2022)

CHAPTER FOUR

PEOPLE & COLLABORATIONS

"I still appreciate
individuality.
Style is much more
interesting than
fashion."

MARC JACOBS,
ON FASHION

MARC JACOBS
JOINS VUITTON

In 1997, Louis Vuitton appointed the American designer Marc Jacobs to join the team as their Creative Director. A hugely gifted designer himself, with a natural instinct for spotting talent, he started working closely with many other designers, architects and artists, introducing the concept of collaborations in fashion – a trend that he has become famous for. Not only did his approach impact Louis Vuitton but the industry at large. He also created the Maison's first prêt-à-porter collection, which positioned the brand at the centre of the French fashion scene.

STEPHEN SPROUSE

In 2001, Marc Jacobs invited the edgy New York artist and fashion designer Stephen Sprouse to collaborate on some Louis Vuitton accessories, something unprecedented at the time. Sprouse, who during the 1980s was described as combining "uptown sophistication in clothing with a downtown punk and pop sensibility", designed freehand graffiti (that read "LOUIS VUITTON PARIS") on the legendary Monogram canvas of several items of luggage, in a sense vandalizing the classic print, but at the same time transforming it. The collection was presented at Louis Vuitton's Spring/Summer 2001 show and made a huge impact.

TRIBUTE COLLECTION

In 2009, this time solely under Marc Jacobs
(Sprouse had died in 2004), a second Sprouse
x Louis Vuitton collaboration was launched.
This tribute collection introduced new colours
of the Monogram graffiti (bright pink,
orange and green) as well as a collection
of rose prints that Sprouse had designed in
2001, on the classic Monogram.

"Grant me the serenity to chill."

STEPHEN SPROUSE,
AS FEATURED ON A TOTE BAG
DESIGNED BY MARC JACOBS IN COLLABORATION
WITH THE SPROUSE ESTATE, 2024

RICHARD PRINCE

Marc Jacobs also enlisted American painter and photographer Richard Prince to collaborate with the Maison in 2008. Known for his abstract paintings and use of appropriation art, he reinterpreted the Monogram by creating a colour version (using 17 different shades) with a soft, delicate watercolour effect, on either a white or a brown background.

"There are no rules. It's one of its problems. But it's also one of the great things about art. It becomes a question of what lasts."

RICHARD PRINCE,
ON ART, 2023

SEX & THE CITY

Prince also designed an abstract collection that was featured in the *Sex and the City* film in 2008. In one of the scenes in the movie, the Richard Prince x Louis Vuitton bag (the Motard Firebird style) is gifted by the main character, Carrie Bradshaw (played by Sarah Jessica Parker), to her assistant Louise (played by Jennifer Hudson) as a thank-you gift.

THE MANCRAZY
JOKES BAG

This limited edition, and highly sought after Richard Prince Louis Vuitton bag is emblazoned with jokes such as: "Every time I meet a girl that cooks like my mother... she looks like my father."

TAKASHI MURAKAMI

Contemporary Japanese artist Takashi Murakami was also approached by Jacobs to collaborate on some of the Louis Vuitton bags. At the time, Murakami had never heard of the brand, and was curious to participate. Known for his "superflat" two-dimensional art, he created his own version of the Monogram using 33 different colours on either a white or a black background. The bags were first seen at the Spring/Summer 2003 Louis Vuitton show, becoming an instant hit, especially with the Speedy, the Alma and the Papillon.

They became a celebrity favourite and were loved by many (including Paris Hilton, Lindsay Lohan and Jessica Simpson). Discontinued in 2015, but in line with the recent noughtie revival, the design has since made a comeback in the vintage market, and has been spotted on Kendall Jenner and Bella Hadid, among others.

ART MEETS FASHION

Murakami's collaborations took place over a period of 12 years, lasting from 2003 until 2015. During this time, he produced a number of screen and mixed media prints, which include Cherry Blossom (2003), Panda (2004), Cerises (2005), MOCA Hands (in 2007, for the Museum of Contemporary Art in Los Angeles exhibition), Monogramouflage (2008) and Cosmic Blossom (2010).

As part of the MOCA exhibition, in 2007 Murakami designed his spectacular Steamer Trunk, which he called the Marilyn. It sold for $500,000, and contained 33 Louis Vuitton x Takashi Murakami monogrammed bags (made of Monogram multicolour canvas, alligator leather and brass) on shelves, positioned at a three-quarter angle. The trunk also featured some drawers on one side. His signature coloured Monogram print covered the exterior of the trunk, which was made of natural cowhide leather, brass and wood. The trunk's dimensions when closed are 39¼ x 22½ x 25½ inches (99.6 x 57.1 x 64.7 cm).

YAYOI KUSAMA

Like Takashi Murakami, Japanese artist Yayoi Kusama wasn't aware of the Louis Vuitton brand when she was first approached by Marc Jacobs. The renowned artist first collaborated with Louis Vuitton in 2012, when she decorated the Monogram with her iconic, repetitive dots, a series she had started painting in the 1970s. Interestingly, this technique, which became her trademark, began as a form of therapy to combat a succession of childhood hallucinations she had experienced from the age of ten.

PUMPKINS & DOTS

Kusama also incorporated variations of Op Art and pumpkin designs on a number of bags, including on classic totes, suitcases, watches and shoes. In 2012, she also famously hand-painted a Louis Vuitton Steamer Trunk using acrylic paint, covering the print with dots in vivid colours: blue, white yellow, green and red.

KUSAMA MONOGRAM

A second, equally successful collaboration, took place in 2023. This time Kusama created some fun flowers, and used more pumpkins and dots to decorate the classic Monogram. This design was featured on clothes, bags (notably on the Speedy and the Alma), suitcases, trunks and shoes. A multi-step serigraphy technique was used to make the finished product look like it was freshly hand-painted.

CAMPAIGN LAUNCH

An impressive campaign launched this collection worldwide: the New York boutique featured a robot of Kusama, while in Paris an inflatable version of the artist was suspended above the store, as if in flight. Meanwhile, in London, the entire façade of department store Harrods was decorated with a colourful projection of the design. A statue of Yayoi Kusama was also displayed inside.

MARC JACOBS – THE FINAL COLLECTION

After 16 years with Louis Vuitton, Marc Jacobs decided to leave the business to concentrate on his eponymous label. His final collection for Louis Vuitton was the Spring/Summer 2014 show, which was publicized with a campaign photographed by Steven Meisel. It featured a series of portraits of his favourite muses: Fan Bingbing, Sofia Coppola, Gisele Bündchen, Catherine Deneuve, Caroline de Maigret and Edie Campbell.

"It was never my desire to revolutionize fashion, to make clothes that could be in a museum. I want to create clothes that have a certain style, but I want to see them used."

MARC JACOBS,
INTERVIEW IN *THE TEEN VOGUE HANDBOOK*, 2009

JEFF KOONS

In 2017, Louis Vuitton collaborated with American artist Jeff Koons (known for his stainless steel balloon-animal sculptures) on two collections. Here, Koons selected several timeless masterpieces – including Leonardo da Vinci's *Mona Lisa* (c. 1503) and Claude Monet's *Water Lilies* (1916) – and printed them on the canvas with his initials and the artist's name on the centre. The Masters collaboration was an interesting concept that brought together established works of art into a new medium, creating a high-end experience of luxury.

KIM JONES

In 2011, Kim Jones was appointed Artistic Director of menswear, reporting to Marc Jacobs. After a successful period at the helm, which included collaborations with New York skate brand Supreme, and artist duo the Chapman Brothers, he stepped down from his role in 2018.

NICOLAS GHESQUIÈRE

Following the departure of Marc Jacobs in 2013, French Designer Nicolas Ghesquière took over as Louis Vuitton's Artistic Director of womenswear. His forward-thinking vision and exceptional technique (he had worked at Balenciaga for 15 years) added a new energy to the Maison, redefining and modernizing the brand's identity. He has designed the renowned Petite Malle bag (a reference to Vuitton's heritage) and the Archlight sneaker (a futuristic trainer with a wave-shaped outsole), among many other classic designs.

"It is a true honour to continue writing the story of Louis Vuitton. We began the first chapter ten years ago, defining a new identity based on extraordinary heritage and a constant focus on innovation."

NICOLAS GHESQUIÈRE,
ON HIS RE-APPOINTMENT AS ARTISTIC DIRECTOR OF
WOMENSWEAR, NOVEMBER 2023

VIRGIL ABLOH

American designer, DJ, artist, architect and founder of the luxury streetwear brand Off-White, Virgil Abloh, joined Louis Vuitton in 2018, replacing Kim Jones. He was the first African-American Artistic Director in charge of menswear at the Maison, and his debut collection, Spring/Summer 2018, was celebrated for its inclusivity (the catwalk had a rainbow projected onto it). The show included a range of styles and covered a myriad of looks, including lots of layering and print, as well as more minimal looks. The presentation was heavily accessorized and included footwear, bags, sunglasses and gloves.

His Autumn/Winter 2021 presentation was perhaps his most notable collection, which explored the concept of streetwear, combining a range of textures and styles (formal and urban) with splashes of colour and accessories, including sunglasses and elegant hats. Abloh sadly died of cancer in 2021, at the age of 41.

"I don't call myself a designer, nor do I call myself an image-maker. I don't reject the label of either. I am not trying to put myself on a pedestal, nor am I trying to be more, now. I would like to define the title of Artistic Director for a new and different era."

VIRGIL ABLOH,
ON HIS DEBUT APPOINTMENT AS ARTISTIC DIRECTOR OF
MENSWEAR, JUNE 2018

"I never thought that it would be me. It was – and it's still – unreal."

PHARRELL WILLIAMS,
ON BEING CHOSEN AS CREATIVE DIRECTOR OF MENSWEAR
AT LOUIS VUITTON, *GQ*, JUNE 2023

PHARRELL WILLIAMS

In 2023, Pharrell Williams joined the Maison as Creative Director of menswear, replacing the late Virgil Abloh. Williams had already collaborated with Louis Vuitton in 2004 to create Millionaires (designing a collection of sunglasses with fashion designer, DJ, drummer and producer Tomoaki Nagao, known as Nigo), and also in 2008, when he designed jewellery for the brand.

THE DEBUT

At his debut show Williams presented tailoring
with a twist by integrating a street aesthetic,
and introduced a new canvas print he called
Damoflage, which combines the traditional
Damier check, originally designed in 1888, with
a camouflage colour palette.

Celebrity front row guests included Jay-Z,
Beyoncé, Maluma, A$AP Rocky, Zendaya,
Lewis Hamilton, Kelly Rowland, Tyler, the
Creator, Kim Kardashian and Rihanna, who
was the face of the Spring/Summer 2024
advertising campaign.

100TH ANNIVERSARY OF THE MONOGRAM CANVAS

The Monogram canvas, a print that has become one of the most iconic and recognizable in fashion history, was designed in 1896 by Georges Vuitton as a tribute to his late father. To mark the centenary of its creation, in 1996 Louis Vuitton invited six prominent fashion designers to come up with new luggage items, which were then exhibited globally as a collection.

The result was an interesting mix: Helmut Lang's slick DJ vinyl box; Sybilla's practical backpack with a built-in umbrella; Romeo Gigli's unusual, pointed hiking bag; Manolo Blahnik's stylish oval shoe trunk; a weekend bag by Isaac Mizrahi; and Vivienne Westwood's eccentric "bustle bag", which could be used a handbag or worn as a backpack when placed in the small of the back.

THE 200TH ANNIVERSARY OF THE BIRTH OF LOUIS VUITTON

To celebrate 200 years since the birth of Monsieur Louis Vuitton, the Maison decorated many of their stores by projecting an image of the founder with the message "Happy Birthday Louis" onto buildings, including boutiques in Singapore's Marina Bay Sands resort, Tokyo's Shibuya and New York's Fifth Avenue.

THE GAME

An interactive online game was also launched
at this time, called "Louis: The Game". Set in
the world of Louis Vuitton, it featured the
Maison's mascot Vivienne – a doll with
a face surrounded by four petals and a
quatre-feuilles eye patch – that had been
launched in 2018.

200 TRUNKS

Another celebration took the form of an extraordinary exhibition called '200 Trunks, 200 Visionaries: The Exhibition', that travelled from Asnières, where Louis Vuitton once worked and lived, all the way to Singapore, then to Los Angeles and finally to New York. The following year an auction took place at Sotheby's. All revenue generated by the auction sale was donated to a Louis Vuitton scholarship programme.

The exhibition showcased the work of 200 artists, each of which was given a blank canvas to design a trunk. The fun collection included works from architect Frank Gehry (his contribution was called *A Tea Party for Louis*), British DJ Benji B's Jukebox Trunk and a black rainbow Monogram Malle Courrier that the late Virgil Abloh had designed for his Spring/Summer 2019 collection.

"There is no household in the world that doesn't have [contact with] Louis Vuitton. There are not a lot of brands that can say they enter the lives of people like we do."

PIETRO BACCARI,
CEO OF LOUIS VUITTON,
FINANCIAL TIMES, MAY 2024